Saint Katharine Drexel

Saint Katharine Drexel

The Total Gift

Written by
Susan Helen Wallace, FSP

Illustrated by
Barbara Kiwak

Pauline
BOOKS & MEDIA
Boston

Library of Congress Cataloging-in-Publication Data

Wallace, Susan Helen, 1940–

   Saint Katharine Drexel : the total gift / written by Susan Helen
Wallace ; illustrated by Barbara Kiwak.

       p. cm. — (Encounter the saints series ; 15)

Summary: A biography of the Philadelphia heiress who surrendered
her life and fortune to God, founding a new congregation of Catholic sisters—the Sisters of the Blessed Sacrament—to minister to the
needs of Native Americans and African Americans.

   ISBN 0-8198-7068-4 (pbk.)

   1. Drexel, Katharine Mary, Saint, 1858-1955—Juvenile literature.
2. Christian women saints—United States—Biography—Juvenile literature. 3. Sisters of the Blessed Sacrament for Indians and Colored
People—Biography—Juvenile literature. [1. Drexel, Katharine Mary,
Saint, 1858-1955. 2. Saints. 3. Women—Biography.] I. Kiwak, Barbara, ill. II. Title. III. Series.

   BX4700.D77 W35 2003

   271'.97—dc21

                                                      2003000076

"P" and Pauline are registered trademarks of the Daughters of St.
Paul.

Copyright © 2003, Daughters of St. Paul

Published by Pauline Books & Media, 50 Saint Pauls Avenue, Boston, MA 02130-3491. www.pauline.org.

Printed in the U.S.A.

SKD VSAUSAPEOILL10-15J12-08888 7068-4

Pauline Books & Media is the publishing house of the Daughters of
St. Paul, an international congregation of women religious serving
the Church with the communications media.

3 4 5 6   16 15 14 13 12

Encounter the Saints Series

Blesseds Jacinta and Francisco Marto
Shepherds of Fatima

Blessed John Paul II
The People's Pope

Blessed Pier Giorgio Frassati
Journey to the Summit

Blessed Teresa of Calcutta
Missionary of Charity

Journeys with Mary
Apparitions of Our Lady

Saint Anthony of Padua
Fire and Light

Saint Bakhita of Sudan
Forever Free

Saint Bernadette Soubirous
And Our Lady of Lourdes

Saint Catherine Labouré
And Our Lady of the Miraculous Medal

Saint Clare of Assisi
A Light for the World

Saint Damien of Molokai
Hero of Hawaii

Saint Edith Stein
Blessed by the Cross

Saint Elizabeth Ann Seton
Daughter of America

Saint Faustina Kowalska
Messenger of Mercy

Saint Frances Xavier Cabrini
Cecchina's Dream

Saint Francis of Assisi
Gentle Revolutionary

Saint Gianna Beretta Molla
The Gift of Life

Saint Ignatius of Loyola
For the Greater Glory of God

Saint Isaac Jogues
With Burning Heart

Saint Joan of Arc
God's Soldier

Saint John Vianney
A Priest for All People

Saint Juan Diego
And Our Lady of Guadalupe

Saint Katharine Drexel
The Total Gift

Saint Martin de Porres
Humble Healer

Saint Maximilian Kolbe
Mary's Knight

Saint Paul
The Thirteenth Apostle

Saint Pio of Pietrelcina
Rich in Love

Saint Teresa of Avila
Joyful in the Lord

Saint Thérèse of Lisieux
The Way of Love

For other children's titles on the saints, visit our Web site:
www.pauline.org.

Contents

1

HANNAH'S GIFT

Francis Drexel and Hannah Langstroth knew that they were meant for each other. Francis studied Hannah's face, looking for the least expression of encouragement. "I don't know how else to say it," he stumbled, "but will you marry me?" Before Hannah could say a word, Francis continued: "We're good for each other. And especially," he added softly, "you're good for me, Hannah." The young woman smiled and answered simply, "Yes, Francis!"

Philadelphia, known as the City of Brotherly Love, was a perfect place for raising a family. Hannah and Francis were married there at Assumption Church on September 28, 1854. Francis was Catholic. His bride was a Baptist Quaker. God and faith were important to them both. The couple's first child, Elizabeth, was born on August 27, 1855. Three years slipped by. Soon Mr. and Mrs. Drexel were happily awaiting the birth of their second child.

Three-year-old Elizabeth was excited too. "Mama, will I have a sister or a brother? May I name the baby?" Elizabeth let her favorite names run through her mind. "When will our new baby get here?" she insisted. She finally received some answers on November 26, 1858, the day her sister was born. "Katharine is a nice name," Elizabeth solemnly approved. Her big eyes widened as she asked, "May I hug the baby?"

"Not yet," Mr. Drexel replied kindly, "she's too little."

Days turned into weeks. And Mrs. Drexel still felt weak and sick. She gazed anxiously at the baby in her arms. "Oh, Katie," she whispered, "I want so much to be part of your growing up." Hannah smiled at the thought of her girls. A simple prayer formed in her mind: *Lord, please let me live!* She repeated the words over and over. They seemed to calm her.

But Hannah's prayer would be answered in a different way. She died just five weeks after Katharine's birth. Her husband wept when he was alone, but he tried to be brave. Elizabeth tiptoed through the big house, wondering what was wrong. Her Papa seemed so quiet and worried. *Where's Mama?* Elizabeth wondered. *I will ask Mama what the problem is.* But the little girl couldn't find her. Finally, Mr. Drexel lifted his daughter onto his lap. His kind eyes were shining with tears.

"What's the matter, Papa?" the little girl asked. "Did you fall and hurt yourself?" Even as he smiled, he wept.

"Something very sad happened to our family today," Mr. Drexel began. "You know that your Mama has been sick, don't you?" Elizabeth nodded her head. "Well, today Mama has gone to heaven to be with Jesus."

"How long will she be gone, Papa?"

"A very long time," her father whispered as he hugged his daughter. "A very long time. But someday we will be with her again."

Mr. Drexel could not have known it at the time, but Hannah had left everyone a gift that would surely have amazed even her. Her second daughter, the baby she loved to hold, was to become a saint of the Catholic Church.

Francis Drexel came home from work every evening with the pressures of the office crowding his mind. He welcomed the eager embraces of his two little girls as Elizabeth, affectionately called Lizzie, filled him in on the events of the day. Mr. Drexel tried his best to be both mother and father to his daughters, but he realized that they needed a mother.

Then Mr. Drexel met Emma Bouvier and her family. In many ways, Emma reminded him of Hannah. The couple dated, and Emma spent time with the children. A year and four months after Hannah's death, Emma and Francis were married on April 10, 1860. They left for a honeymoon to Europe, and Uncle Anthony Drexel and his wife took care of Katharine and Elizabeth. When Francis and Emma Drexel returned home, the girls were anxiously waiting. "Isn't she pretty?" Lizzie whispered. "I hope she likes us!" Katharine giggled in reply. The couple rushed up to the children and hugged and kissed them. Emma felt she truly could be a mother to the little girls, and she would be.

When Katharine was old enough to understand whom her real mother was, she loved and cherished Hannah's memory. Many years later, when Katharine—then Mother Katharine—was sixty-five years old, something unusual happened. An employee of the Drexel Company brought her a small box that had been found in an unused company safe. It was believed that the box had belonged to her father and uncle. No one at the Drexel Company knew the combination, and the box was securely locked. Nitroglycerine was finally used to blow it open. Among the treasures inside were keepsakes that had belonged to Hannah. Mother Katharine fingered the small objects lovingly: a gold thimble, gold lorgnette (reading glasses on a stick), jewels and cards with Hannah's name and address. The nun touched the objects reverently. She decided that the gold and jeweled treasures would be used to make a chalice and sacred vessels for priests to use at Mass.

After ill health had forced Mother Katharine to retire from her years of activity for God, she spent long hours daily in the convent chapel. As she thought about her family, she prayed lovingly for her birth mother. Her father and Emma were buried in the family crypt at Torresdale, Pennsylvania. Would it be possible to have the remains of her birth mother, Hannah, moved there? She asked Philadelphia's archbishop, Cardinal Dougherty, for permission. He graciously granted it and the remains of Hannah Drexel were reverently moved from the Cemetery of the Brethren in Germantown, Pennsylvania, to the Drexel crypt. Mother Katharine was overjoyed.

2

LIFE ON WALNUT STREET

The sound of children's footsteps skipping and running across the hardwood floors was ordinary in the Drexel home. When they were tired of hide and seek, it was time to play house.

"Maybe I can be the Mommy today," Kate said hopefully. "Then I can pick the room that will be our *house*. And," she added triumphantly, "I can make you do your homework!"

Lizzie frowned. "But I'm three years older than you!" she protested. "That means *I* get to be in charge."

Good natured Kate shrugged her shoulders. "Okay," she agreed. "Someday I'll be grown up like you anyway. Then I can be the boss."

The years passed quickly. Katharine and her older sister were good company for each other. During the winter months, *home* was on Philadelphia's fashionable Walnut Street. During the summer, the family rented a big farm in Nicetown, Pennsylvania. Summer or winter, Mr. Drexel was busy at his banking firm. He willingly gave his new wife a free hand to turn their city home into a practical place for raising a family. Emma thoroughly enjoyed her role. She had a way with the household staff, and she was fitting right in.

Mrs. Drexel seemed also to understand the ready-made family she had inherited on her wedding day. She and her husband were deeply religious. Despite their wealth both appreciated a simple lifestyle. Emma surrounded her children with reminders of their Catholic faith. One room in the house was even turned into a family chapel. Throughout the house were religious pictures, crucifixes and statues. The children grew up in a decidedly Catholic atmosphere.

Elizabeth and Katharine were overjoyed when their sister, Louise, was born on October 2, 1863, the feast of the Guardian Angels. Mrs. Drexel smilingly confided, "Louise is our gift from the angels." Katharine, nearly five, and now answering to the name "Kate," stared at the lovely baby. All of her life, Kate would refer to Louise as "my little sister."

The Drexel family had the custom of saying night prayers together. Parents and children gathered in their chapel for this important time. The girls also began to attend

*The family had the custom of
saying night prayers together.*

classes at the nearby Convent of the Sacred Heart. School was challenging and fun at the same time. Kate was eager to learn to read, print and write. She was also anxious to try her hand at letter and composition writing.

"I like to write letters," Kate announced to her family. "When you put words down on paper, they become easier to understand and harder to forget." Kate often wrote short notes to Emma. Her mother kept these treasured letters in a little pile, tied with a ribbon. One of them, from six-year-old Kate, reads:

Dear Mama:

Happy Birthday…. May the Blessed Mother send you a kiss from Heaven.

Your affectionate little daughter,

Kate

Another, from a later date, declares:

I am going to make my First Communion and you will see how I shall try to be good. Let me make it in May, the most beautiful of all months.

Kate Drexel who loves you

Kate grew up before the time of Pope Saint Pius X, the Pope who permitted children to receive Communion at a younger age. And so she had to wait until she was eleven to make her First Holy Communion. The wonderful day finally came—June 3, 1870. Kate said little about her experience on that actual day, but kept the memory alive in her heart. Years later, as a nun, she wrote in her retreat notes about her First Communion: "Jesus made me shed tears because of his greatness in stooping to me. *Truth* made me feel the *mite* I was…." Kate felt very close to Jesus in the Holy Eucharist. This feeling would remain and grow all her life.

Kate had so many questions that no one seemed able to answer. *Why am I happy sometimes and sad other times? Why are some people rich and some people poor? Why do bad things happen to good people? Jesus will understand my questions*, she thought as she headed for the family chapel. She loved to make brief visits to Jesus. Even though the Holy Eucharist was not kept in the chapel, the room was special, and Kate felt the presence of God there. She also loved to go to her parish church for the celebration of the Eucharist.

Kate learned a lot about prayer from her father. After greeting each member of the family when he arrived home from work in the evening, he would climb the stairs to his room. There he spent half an hour or so praying and meditating. This fascinated Kate. "Papa, how do you meditate?" she asked. Mr. Drexel smiled. "I think about God's goodness and love for us," he explained kindly. "I remind myself of how God has everything in his heart. He takes care of our family, my work, everything. I tell him that I trust him totally." Kate's wide eyes glowed as she sat intrigued by her father's words.

3

LEARNING TO HELP

Kate's world and interests widened constantly. Every Sunday, after Mass, Mr. Drexel took Elizabeth and Kate to visit Grandma and Grandpa Bouvier, Mrs. Drexel's parents. Then it was on to Grandma Drexel's, Mr. Drexel's mother. His father, Francis Martin Drexel, had been killed in an accident. Grandma Drexel must have appreciated those family visits that filled her lonely hours.

The two older Drexel girls had a "bonus" grandmother, whom they called Grandma Langstroth. They couldn't quite understand why they had three grandmothers and their youngest sister, Louise, had only two, but they loved all their grandparents. They spent Saturdays with Grandmother Langstroth, playing with their cousins and enjoying the wonderful toys their third grandmother provided for them.

Years later, Kate–Mother Katharine–smiled as she recalled that some Saturdays

Grandma and Grandpa Langstroth's Quaker minister joined them for dinner and supper. The first time it happened, Lizzie and Kate watched and listened as Grandma asked the minister to offer the blessing before the meal. Lizzie began to get nervous. She had never met or prayed with a minister before. She promptly decided how to handle the situation and whispered instructions to Kate. During the minister's prayer, the two little girls held up their rosaries to show that they were Catholics!

Lizzie, Kate, and Louise loved beautiful clothes. At the change of seasons, Mrs. Drexel would take them to the Convent of the Good Shepherd. The sisters there sewed clothing for families. During one visit Elizabeth, Kate, and Louise heard their mother specify to the sister in charge that each of the dresses was to be *plain*. Katharine whispered to herself, "Oh, no!"

Mrs. Drexel chose the materials and waited patiently until the girls were measured. Everything was arranged and the family headed toward the door. But Kate hadn't given up. Quickly she ran back to the sister seamstress and took her by the hand. "Please," she pleaded, "do put lots of lace and ruffles on my dress, just like Mama's!"

Kate and her sisters were born into wealth, but their parents were determined to teach their children how to be unselfish. Mrs. Drexel took it upon herself to assist the many poor people in her home city of Philadelphia. She knew how to explain to her daughters that the money and gifts they had received were given them by God to share with those less fortunate. The little girls were to see this belief lived out in their parents' example, and helping the less fortunate would become a normal part of their growing up.

The poor in those days suffered greatly. Scores of young women had lost their husbands in the Civil War, which had ended that year, 1865. Others were ill or injured and unable to work. People all over the country were talking about America's great need for healing. Binding the wounds of prejudice, poverty, and ignorance would be the work of many heroes. Persons of courage were needed to step forward and do their part to rebuild a nation founded on love. Then, and only then, would the Civil War *really* be won. Little Kate Drexel would grow up to become just such a person....

Mrs. Drexel set aside three afternoons each week for her charitable work. "Mama,"

Kate would ask hopefully, "may I help you when the poor people come? I'll smile and make them feel welcome."

"Of course you can help," her mother would proudly answer, giving Kate a hug. "After all, you're nearly seven now."

Kate stood right by her mother. She met each person who came to their door in need of food or clothing. Kate looked into their faces. She saw pain and sadness. Often tears filled her eyes. The little girl watched and listened. Kate realized that she was just a child, but she also realized that God had blessed her in many ways. She was glad she could help.

Mrs. Drexel listened to each needy person and offered sympathy along with rent money, clothing, and medicine. Young Kate was impressed.

The same kind of example helped in the making of another saint, Therese of Lisieux from France. Her father, Louis Martin, lived at the same time as Emma Drexel. Mr. Martin set aside Monday afternoons for helping those in need. People lined up at his door, trusting in his goodness. Mr. Martin offered them food, clothing, money, and even job recommendations. Young Therese, who helped her father, learned from him how to put love into practice. Kate learned the same lesson from her mother.

4

HAPPY MEMORIES

Emma Drexel was a very thorough woman. She wanted the best for her daughters—the best in everything.

"Why don't we have the girls tutored here at home?" she suggested to her husband one day. "That's fine with me," he replied, looking up from the morning paper. "Do you have any teachers in mind?"

"As a matter of fact, I do," his wife came back with a smile.

Mrs. Drexel soon hired Mr. Michael Cross to teach piano. Professor Allen and his daughter, Bessie, would teach Latin; Justin Clave, French. Things were off to a very good start, but Mrs. Drexel still needed a tutor for the overall instruction of her daughters. She wanted someone who would also serve as a good role model for her girls. Emma's sister, a Religious of the Sacred Heart, recommended Mary Ann Cassidy of Camden, New Jersey. Miss Cassidy met with the Drexels. They liked her and hired her for the position.

Life was interesting for Kate, and she was growing quickly. She would have her twelfth birthday in 1870, the year Miss Cassidy came into her life. Miss Cassidy was a warm, lively young woman with a thick Irish brogue. The girls wanted to hear the story of why she had come to America. After a bit of coaxing, Mary Ann began: "I came to America with my parents and sister. We love Ireland, of course. It's our homeland, but life was hard there. We were so poor. You often hear about people with dreams, don't you?" She looked at the eager young faces before her. "Well, we Cassidy's had a dream, too. We wanted to come to America where we could work our way out of poverty. We brought almost nothing else with us but that dream."

The girls never moved as the story continued. Kate had all she could do to keep back her tears. "Shortly after we arrived," Miss Cassidy continued, "something totally unexpected happened. My father died. We were very sad to lose him. I was the oldest child, and the support of the family then fell on my shoulders. So I worked part time and went to school to become a teacher. There's a lot more to the story, but we'll leave that for another time."

The girls were quiet. Katie was dying to ask questions, but she didn't want to pry. The bond between the Drexel sisters and their teacher would deepen. Miss Cassidy had been the ideal choice.

Mrs. Drexel worked hard to prepare a classroom equipped with desks, pictures, maps, reference, and textbooks. The *Drexel School* with a total enrollment of three began. As the days passed, Miss Cassidy introduced her students to literature and philosophy. They began courses in letter writing, composition, public speaking and manners. They learned Church history, world history and Latin. School couldn't exactly be considered fun, but Kate had to admit that it was interesting and even exciting at times.

Mr. Drexel followed his girls' education with genuine interest. Listening to his daughters' supper conversations, he realized how eager they were to study history. They were especially anxious to learn about the brief history of their own United States.

"Well," Mr. Drexel asked one day, "what could be more effective than to show you firsthand the places you're reading about and locating on maps? What if each summer we go as a family to visit some historical site or 'geographic' wonder? On my business trips I've seen the beauty of our country. I want you to see it, too. Sound good?"

Excitement lit the girls' faces. "Yes!" they exclaimed. Their father beamed.

Every fall Mr. Drexel also took his family on a two-week vacation. In other words, the *summer* trips were for learning and the *fall* trips were for relaxing. The vacation trips took them to parts of New England, such as the White Mountains of New Hampshire. Other years they went to California, Colorado, the Great Lakes area, and New Orleans, Louisiana. The girls were storing up many happy memories.

In 1870, Mr. Drexel bought a ninety-acre farm in Torresdale, Pennsylvania. The farm was to be a summer country home for the family. The large house was completely remodeled under Mrs. Drexel's skillful direction. Cottages were built for the staff and their families. A stable, carriage house, and barn were erected. A large statue of Saint Michael the Archangel was placed over the main entrance of the Drexel home. This was an Emma Drexel touch. She also had a stained glass window installed at the first landing of the elegant staircase inside the home. Saint Michael was definitely put in charge. Everything was ready by June of

1871. The house would be called *Saint Michel's* (pronounced: *Sant Mi – shell's*) in French. The family affectionately called their new home "the Nest."

The whole family loved Saint Michel's. The girls were especially anxious to spend their summers there. In time they were given responsibilities for "the Nest's" upkeep. Elizabeth was in charge of the kitchen and stable. Kate was housekeeper and supervisor of employees. Louise watched over the farm, garden, and the dogs. The girls, under their mother's supervision, also taught catechism classes to the children of their employees and neighbors. Kate loved this best of all.

5

THE GRAND TOUR

The school year of 1874 promised to be out of the ordinary. Kate was going on sixteen and ready for an exciting adventure. And Mr. and Mrs. Drexel had one in the planning. They wanted to take their daughters on a tour of Europe.

In those pre-jet days, the family was to travel by ship. The girls were thrilled. The Drexels and Johanna Ryan, their colorful Irish maid, boarded the *Scotia,* an ocean liner, in New York Harbor that September. They would be gone until the following May!

Mr. Drexel had mapped out a trip through several countries. Miss Cassidy, on the home front, expected to receive two letters a week about their adventures from each of her pupils. Lizzie and Louise knew that Kate would be the letter writer. Nobody but Kate could find so many good things to say about a cathedral, a statue, a fountain. Yes, Kate would be their roving reporter.

Their ship landed in Liverpool, England, much to the agitation of Johanna, affectionately called "Joe" by the Drexels. How could a gorgeous ship like the *Scotia* chose to dock in England rather than Ireland? Oh, if only the Drexels could see her native Ireland, they would be in for an unforgettable treat. And wouldn't Joe be delighted to take on the role of tour guide? But it wasn't to be. England it was.

"My only consolation," Joe muttered, "is that our visit to England will last but a single day." The girls laughed. The family spent that day sightseeing at Westminster Abbey where English kings and queens had been crowned and buried since 1066.

"Joe, you're welcome to stay here at the hotel and rest," Mrs. Drexel said kindly. "I know you might not be very interested in Westminster Abbey." The girls watched Joe's lively eyes. They knew what she would do.

"I might as well come, seeing I'm here," the maid answered quickly.

The visitors saw the magnificent tomb of King Saint Edward I, called Edward the Confessor. (Confessor, in this sense, means a person who loves, teaches, and defends his faith.)

The tourists stopped for a few minutes before the tomb of Queen Elizabeth I, daughter of Henry VIII. During her sixteenth century reign, she had claimed the ancient Westminster Abbey for the new Anglican Church. Kate was impressed with the history of this cathedral that had been Catholic until Reformation times. There was much to reflect on during their brief visit. The Catholic faith in England ran deep and the martyrs were plentiful. Kate wished that she and her family could return some day to England and stay longer.

The group moved on to Lausanne, Switzerland next. Mr. Drexel had arranged that an old family friend from Baltimore meet them there. Miss Carrere, "Caro," as the girls called her, knew the country well. She had been living in Europe for many years. Caro served as tour guide for this part of the trip.

Vienna, Austria would be unforgettable to the two older girls but for an unusual reason. Lizzie and Kate had decided to go to the nearest Catholic church and receive the sacrament of Reconciliation. The girls started out one morning, clinging to their guidebooks. Their plan seemed simple enough, but was to prove otherwise. Finally arriving at Saint Catherine's Church, they blurted out a few German phrases to the old caretaker. But he couldn't understand what they were saying and slammed the door on them. In the end, it was their French lessons that saved the day. Lizzie and Kate managed to stumble through their confession in French at a nearby Franciscan monastery.

Now it was on to Italy. Kate's excitement mounted. She wanted to see the Pope and the Vatican. "Can we *please* also stop in Assisi?" she begged her parents. "I've always loved Saint Francis." Kate was hard to refuse when she really wanted something, which only rarely happened. But her parents had other factors to consider, and the visit to Assisi never materialized.

Upon their arrival in Italy, the family stayed overnight in Bologna. Mr. Drexel was anxious to visit Rome and Florence. On November 26, 1874, Kate celebrated her sixteenth birthday. The Drexels spent Christmas in Naples.

New Year, 1875, began in Rome. An audience with the Pope was arranged. The Drexels presented Pope Pius IX, now Blessed Pius IX, with a white skullcap. Louise made the presentation and asked His Holiness for his skullcap in return. The Pope placed it playfully on the little girl's head. Joe, overcome with emotion, knelt and en-

Louise presented their gift to the Pope.

thusiastically threw her arms around the Pope's legs. All too soon the papal audience was over and on its way to becoming a wonderful memory. Reluctantly, the Drexels concluded their visit to Italy and headed for France. Kate hadn't been able to visit Assisi, but she could be patient. She hoped she would someday have another chance. In the meantime, she felt a longing in the depths of her heart, a kind of gentle, persistent restlessness. What did it mean? She would go to Jesus and ask him.

6
FIREWORKS!

The year Kate turned 18, 1876, was also the Centennial year for Americans—the 100th anniversary of the signing of the Declaration of Independence. Philadelphia was planning a whole year of Centennial celebrations. It was all so exciting.

"Parades," Lizzie sighed, "I just love them!"

"So do I," Louise added dreamily. Before Kate could give her opinion, Mr. Drexel broke in. "You'll have to wear warm coats and gloves. It's very cold outside."

"Our country has packed a lot of history into 100 years," Kate thought aloud. "Wouldn't you like to look ahead and see what America will be like on its 200th anniversary?"

"I can tell you one thing for sure, Kate," said her father with a grin, "none of us will be around to see it." The girls laughed.

"In 1976 who will remember that we Drexels ever even lived?" Lizzie asked thoughtfully. The clamor of the crowd drowned out the rest of their conversation.

The official Centennial opening was set for May 10, but the festivities would begin that night, New Year's Eve. It was time for the Drexels to leave for the parade. Fireworks lit the night sky in the distance. "Beautiful! Wonderful!" the girls exclaimed.

But there was a different kind of fireworks going on in Kate's heart. As the days passed, she wondered what direction her life should take. Kate had a spiritual director, Father James O'Connor, who was guiding her in her spiritual life. He had been the pastor of the parish in which Saint Michel's was located. Kate trusted him. She could speak her heart's thoughts, fears, and hopes to him. She could ask him for guidance about important issues, like God's plan for her life.

Kate felt as if a road was opening for her through a forest tangled with vines. She saw Father O'Connor as the one who would lead her. During the four years he had known Kate, he had helped her to grow in her love of Jesus. God had a special plan for Kate, but she could never have guessed what it was....

Kate recorded her thoughts and feelings in her diary. She talked to her diary as if it were a friend. *A diary's a good listener,* she thought. *When I write things down, they somehow become clearer.*

Kate finished school on July 2, 1878, and spent the summer at Saint Michel's. Her good friend, Father O'Connor, had been named Bishop of Omaha, Nebraska, but his letters kept coming to encourage and guide her.

On January 1, 1879, Kate was given a special party, called a debut, by her parents. This was her formal invitation to join the social life of the privileged young men and women of Philadelphia. The Drexel home had never looked more beautiful. The girls hadn't either. Louise, who would be sixteen in October, glowed with excitement. Guests soon began arriving. Mr. Drexel looked pleased, but parties were not his specialty. His wife was definitely in charge and enjoying every minute of it.

"Your mother looks stunning, Louise," Mr. Drexel said. "And you do, too. All my girls are especially beautiful tonight. By the way, where is Kate?"

"She's still getting ready," Louise responded with a bit of impatience.

Kate finally slipped quietly into the dining room. After her parents proudly presented her to their guests, she politely mingled with the visitors. Kate summed up the entire event in a single sentence in a letter she wrote to Bishop O'Connor three days later: "I attended a little party the other night where I made my debut." What was *really* going on inside of her?

The year moved ahead. Kate and Elizabeth spent the summer at Saint Michel's as usual. In between, they enjoyed parties at the homes of relatives and family friends. Everyone went out of their way to entertain the girls. At each place they visited, they were the center of attention. The adults sat or stood around the edges of the room sipping their punch and watching the wealthy young men shower their attention on the Drexel sisters.

Liz and Kate seemed to be enjoying themselves, but they saved plenty of time for writing letters to their family. "Francis," Mrs. Drexel said after supper one evening. "Just look at the length of these letters from the girls, several pages each. Why, they might as well come home and tell us everything in person!" Mr. Drexel smiled. "It is nice to be missed, isn't it?"

"Of course," his wife responded, "but we want them to socialize, too, dear, and meet some nice young men. The years fly by so quickly; our girls are growing up."

In spite of all the fun and excitement, Kate and Liz were homesick. They missed their family. It was time to go home.

7

PEACE IN SUFFERING

"Mama, you're pale today," Kate said softly. "How are you feeling?"

"Tired, to tell you the truth, dear," Mrs. Drexel replied. "This hot weather always slows me down a bit." But even the relaxing atmosphere of Saint Michel's did nothing to improve her health, so Mrs. Drexel made a quiet visit to her doctor back in Philadelphia.

"You need a minor operation," he concluded. "It can be done right in your home on Walnut Street. Don't worry. You'll be back to your old self in no time." That was just what Mrs. Drexel was hoping to hear.

When the day for the operation came, she casually told her family that she and one of the maids had to go into the city on business. No one at Saint Michel's thought anything of it. Mrs. Drexel hid the planned operation from her family because she didn't want to worry them. But the procedure was not so simple when the surgeon found cancer....

Francis Drexel, confused and shaken, hurried to his wife's side. She looked so tiny and pale in the sea of white bed sheets.

"Emma, why didn't you tell me?" he whispered tearfully. Mrs. Drexel reached up and patted her husband's cheek. "I wanted to spare you the worry and pain," she said weakly. Tears filled her own eyes as she realized that this had not been the case.

Slowly 1879 dissolved into 1880. Mr. Drexel called in all the best doctors. But medicine could do only so much. Mr. Drexel even took his wife on a trip to Colorado hoping that her health would improve, but she returned as ill as ever. Emma Drexel experienced terrible pain as the cancer made its way through her body. She suffered heroically all during 1881. It was her faith that gave her the courage to battle her illness with such dignity. Seized by moments of agonizing pain, she often said to her husband: "Oh Frank, how I pray that when your time comes, you will be spared all this. And now I offer this pain I suffer for you."

Mrs. Drexel suffered for three long years. During that time Kate was her tender and conscientious nurse. In the long hours she spent by her mother's bedside, the young woman had plenty of time to think about the deeper side of life. She was amazed at her mother's genuine acceptance of God's will. Kate saw an optimism in her mother that could not be crushed by even the most horrible sufferings. *When it's my turn to die,* she reflected, *what will it matter that I've had a fancy debut? The only thing that will matter then is how I've spent my life. Oh Lord,* Kate prayed, *help me to be generous like my mother!*

Mrs. Drexel hung on to life during Christmas, 1882, but it would be her last. She died on January 29, 1883. The family's grief was deep. Word spread throughout the city. People flocked to the Drexel home the day before the funeral. The single line of mourners passed continuously by Emma Drexel's open casket. Many whom she had helped came just to say thank you.

After the funeral, the family retreated to their home to mourn. Mr. Drexel went to his room and played the organ for hours. This was his way of voicing his grief. The organ recital was for Emma.

8

Unexpected Sorrow

As 1883 dragged along, Mr. Drexel gradually returned to his normal daily routine. His daughters took over the household responsibilities. The three sisters had always been close. Now they became even closer, bound by their deep loss.

"Do you hear her, too?" Kate asked. "I keep hearing Mama walking down the halls, humming happily as she used to."

"I know," Liz mumbled, "This big house is empty without her." Louise shrugged in agreement. Mr. Drexel felt it, too. The kindly man realized that he had to do something.

"It's time for another trip," Mr. Drexel announced to his daughters one day. It was early in October of 1883 when they sailed for Europe. Faithful Miss Cassidy would manage the home while the family was away. The Drexels visited Holland, Germany, Italy, France and England. The three sisters wrote enthusiastic letters back home. They didn't return to Philadelphia until May of 1884.

Summer flew by at Saint Michel's, and with the coming of September, Mr. Drexel had trip number two mapped out. This time they traveled by railroad to the Northwest. Kate was excited. She wanted to see as much of America as she could. The Drexels traveled in their own private railroad car. Mr. Drexel was combining business with pleasure. He wanted to judge for himself whether the Northern Pacific Railroad would be a good investment for his company. To help him in this decision Mr. Drexel brought along two members of his business firm. He also brought his niece, Elizabeth Dixon, whose mother had recently died. The group was pleasant company and the scenery was beautiful. The party journeyed from Torresdale, Pennsylvania to Portland, Oregon, with a detour to Yellowstone National Park. Kate tabulated the distance of the entire trip and recorded it in her diary: 6,833 miles!

One evening after returning home, Mr. Drexel gathered his daughters together. "I feel I've done a good day's work today," he announced. "I think you'll be pleased." The three sisters glanced at each other. Their father was acting mysteriously.

"What kind of work?" one of the girls prodded.

"I've made my will," their father quietly replied.

Kate felt a chill run through her. With her mother's recent death, she just couldn't face the thought of losing her father.

In February of 1885, less than a year after their return from Europe, Mr. Drexel caught a cold that developed into pleurisy. His doctors felt confident that he would recover, however. Elizabeth took charge of his medications, and all three girls took turns serving as his nurse. Mr. Drexel responded well to the love and care and seemed to be recovering nicely. On Sunday, February 15, he spent an hour in silent prayer. Later that morning, he was quietly reading. Kate was doing the same in the adjoining room. At a certain point, Kate looked up. Through the doorway she saw her father stand and begin to walk toward her. But suddenly he slumped back into the chair. His eyes were glassy and his face was bathed in perspiration. "Elizabeth! Louise! Something's happened to Papa! Call the doctor!" Kate cried as she sped down the stairs. "I'm going to St. Patrick's for a priest!"

The housekeeper at St. Patrick's rectory immediately responded to Kate's anxious ringing. Beside herself with worry, Kate rushed past the woman and burst into the parlor, where a group of priests were having a meeting. "Come quickly!" she pleaded. "My father is dying!" None of the stunned priests moved. After a few seconds that seemed to Kate like an eternity, one priest stood. "I'll come," he answered kindly.

Meanwhile, a quick-thinking Drexel employee arrived at the rectory. "I heard you tell your sisters to call a doctor," the woman explained, "so I took a cab to Saint John's and got a priest. The cab driver is here now to pick you up."

Kate hurried home to find that her father had just died. Everyone in the house was in shock. Elizabeth, Kate, and Louise were once again clothed in grief. Archbishop Ryan celebrated the funeral Mass at Mr. Drexel's parish church, Saint Mary's. The overflow crowd of 2,000 mourners was a real testimony to his goodness.

Yet, even all the love and sympathy shown to the family seemed a small consolation. After the funeral, when the crowds had gone home, the Drexel sisters remained alone with their sorrow.

9

Friend of the Missions

Not long after Mr. Drexel's death, his daughters studied his will carefully. "We have work to do," Liz said, raising her eyebrows.

"A lot of work," Louise seconded.

"I'm not surprised at all the charitable causes Papa provided for," Kate remarked with admiration. "This will just continues the way our parents spent their lives. It provides plenty for each of us and lets us help Papa help others."

"The best thing we can do," Liz agreed, "is to begin to help the poor and make their lives easier."

As the girls got to work, their personal loneliness over the loss of their parents became easier to bear. Each of the sisters adopted a particular charitable cause they would help for as long as each lived. The girls sought trusted advice in financial management, as their father had taught them. They wanted to become good businesswomen for the sake of the many needy people who would profit by their father's fortune.

Elizabeth, the oldest, and often the first to walk down new and challenging paths, chose to continue her father's dedication to various orphanages. But she wanted to carry it one step further. She planned to build an orphanage that would continue the youngsters' education after their elementary school training was completed. She clearly saw the need for a school where young people would learn a useful trade. Elizabeth bought property and oversaw the building of the Saint Francis de Sales Industrial School for young men. Liz regularly toured the construction site noting the details and checking the progress. After all, this school was to be a memorial to her father. Archbishop Ryan blessed the completed building on July 28, 1888. Saint Francis de Sales would offer thousands of young men the skilled training they needed to help them make a profitable living as adults.

Louise's main concern was to ease the plight of African Americans. She gave large amounts of money to the Josephite Fathers, a religious congregation dedicated to serving the needs of African Americans. Louise purchased property in Baltimore for the Josephite Fathers and donated money toward the establishment of their Epiphany College. In 1889, Louise married Colonel Edward Morrell. The couple continued Louise's charitable works. They built Saint Emma's Industrial and Agricultural Institute, a school of higher learning and training for young African American men.

Kate directed her concern to both Native Americans and African Americans. She was made vividly aware of the poverty of the Indians because of two special visitors who came to the Drexel home. One afternoon before Louise's marriage, the girls were upstairs when the butler announced the arrival of two priests. The sisters looked at each other. No guests were expected. Louise turned to Kate. "You go down," she said with authority. Kate cheerfully obliged, totally unaware that this meeting would change her life forever.

The visitors were missionaries from the Indian territories. They were Bishop Martin Marty, a Benedictine from Minnesota, and Father Joseph Stephan, Director of the Bureau of Catholic Indian Missions. Kate immediately felt at home with the two missionaries. She listened carefully as a whole new area of human suffering opened before her. The missionaries explained the plight of the

American Indian. These men had spent years among the Native Americans. Kate realized that they shared the Native Americans' poverty and burdens. Time seemed to stop as Kate listened and pictured in her imagination the squalor and misery the two priests spoke of. An uneasy feeling came over her. Her great heart seemed to burst with the need to do something. That day began her lifelong relationship with the American Indians.

While the two visitors had refreshments, Kate went upstairs for her checkbook. She would begin by giving money. But that wasn't enough to satisfy her longing to help. "I know you have wonderful causes," Kate pleaded with her sisters, "but won't you help the Indians, too? Their poverty cuts at the heart." Her sisters chuckled. Somehow they realized that they would always be involved in Kate's work as well as their own.

By 1907, the Drexel sisters had donated a million and a half dollars. And the giving continued. Kate asked the missionaries for reports of how her money was spent. She read them carefully to make sure the donations were reaching the people she intended to help. She realized that she was merely the keeper of a part of her father's

*"The Native Americans are
in great need, Miss Drexel."*

fortune. She never wanted people to think that she was the benefactor. "I want to be anonymous," she would explain. "Please don't use my name. Just call me a "friend of the missions."

10

"WHY NOT YOU?"

Elizabeth and Louise couldn't help noticing that Kate wasn't well. She had lost weight and frequently felt ill. Lizzie and Louise decided that it was time for another tour of Europe. This would be the best medicine. They boarded the *S.S. Ambria* on July 31, 1886. The trip through Europe went ahead at a leisurely pace so as not to tire Kate. She improved steadily. Color gradually returned to her cheeks and she no longer had to push herself to join in the delightful excursions. She began to enjoy herself.

Meanwhile, a steady stream of letters followed the recovering young woman. Father Stephan and other priests serving the Native Americans sent detailed accounts of the missions she was helping. For someone so young and new to charity work, Kate seemed to take to it naturally. She had never lived in an Indian village, but she grasped the problems the priests' letters explained and instinctively understood the needs of the Native people. Kate loved to hear from the missionaries. She felt part of a great and valuable work. She and her sisters shared the good news of progress, spiritual and material, among the Native Americans. The priests also confided the challenges, too.

"A difficulty more serious than the lack of money," they told her, "is the lack of priests and nuns to serve the people." What was going on inside of twenty-eight year old Kate? Could God be calling *her* to serve in some way?

Since the matter was urgent, young Kate decided there was no harm in asking the one person who could do something about the problem. Years later, Mother Katharine recalled: "We went to Rome and had a private audience with Pope Leo XIII. Kneeling at his feet, I thought that surely God's Vicar would not refuse me. So I pleaded for missionary priests for the American Indians. To my astonishment His Holiness responded, 'Why not become a missionary yourself, my child?'"

Often enough, the thought of a vocation to religious life had passed through Kate's mind. But this was different. She was stunned by the Pope's direct question. The possibility of her own vocation surfaced with the impact of a jet slamming into a mountain. When her audience with Pope Leo was ended, Kate went back into Saint Peter's and felt suddenly ill. She rushed from the huge church, sobbing her heart out while her perplexed sisters stood quietly by.

Kate began to pray and think about her call to religious life. She went over everything in her mind. First, she considered a hidden religious life. She hungered for God in a life of prayer, contemplation, and Eucharistic devotion. Secondly, she definitely wanted to serve the Native and African Americans. Thirdly, she wanted to use her fortune to provide for their needs.

Kate asked advice especially from her trusted friend, Bishop James O'Connor. She had to take the next step toward her goal and enter religious life. But how? Bishop O'Connor wrote from Omaha, Nebraska, on February 16, 1889. He leaned toward having Kate begin a new religious congregation in the Church. Kate was overwhelmed by the idea. Wouldn't it be better to join an already existing community of sisters? As a foundress, she would have to set the example for her community. In fact, she would have to *be* the example. At this thought, Kate didn't know whether to laugh or cry. She wanted to see the bishop and

Father Stephen in person. Could they come for a brief visit?

Bishop O'Connor was sure of God's plan for Kate. "I have never been as sure of any vocation, even my own, as I am of yours," he wrote. "If you do not establish this new congregation, you will allow a great opportunity to pass by." The bishop's letter continued. He patiently eliminated, one by one, the obstacles Kate had outlined in her previous letter. "I regard it as settled that you are to establish a new congregation of sisters," the bishop concluded, "and I shall go to Philadelphia merely to arrange the details. The Church has spoken to you through me...."

In his enthusiasm, Bishop O'Connor confided the plan for the new congregation to Archbishop Ireland of Chicago. The archbishop was very excited about it. Kate was happy and sad, relieved and anxious. All she could do now was to trust that everything was the work of the Holy Spirit. She whispered good-bye to her dream of a cloistered life and turned decisively toward her calling to begin a new religious community rooted in the Eucharistic Jesus. Kate and the vocations God would send would bring the love of Jesus to the Native and African Americans.

Kate had to be trained as a religious sister. Bishop O'Connor suggested that she receive her instruction from the Sisters of Mercy in Pittsburgh. Kate and Elizabeth visited the sisters in April. They were very welcoming, and the Drexels liked what they saw. The following month, on May 6, 1889, Kate joined the convent. The recently married Louise, her husband, Colonel Morrell, and Elizabeth accompanied her. In the train station, the three sisters hugged. This was to be, in many ways, a new beginning for them.

11

No Turning Back

Kate eyed the long, dimly lit hallways and bare floors of the convent. She sighed happily. At last she was on her way to becoming a sister!

I've got to get into a whole new routine, she thought. *I guess I'll be moved along by the sound of a bell.* Now dressed in her black postulant's uniform, Kate looked down at the plain dress. *Ah, I still miss those ruffles,* she mused. *But one thing is sure: I promise myself to find humor and joy in my new life.*

I can hardly believe this is happening, she reflected as she followed the others to the next duty. *Even more, I can't believe I'm able to adjust so easily to this life. It's definitely the Lord's doing.* As she made her way to chapel, Kate silently prayed: *Dear Jesus, I want to give my whole self to you.*

This time spent with the Sisters of Mercy was to prepare Kate to belong totally to Jesus. She approached her convent training with openness and trust. During sewing sessions, for example, the novices would mend their own stockings and other articles of clothing by hand. Kate remembered the expensive clothes hanging in her closets back home. She fingered her black stockings and grinned as she darned.

Obedience, too, was important in Kate's preparation for religious life. She willingly accepted the guidance of the sisters in charge. It was not difficult for her. What she did still struggle with was the terrifying thought that she was in training not only to be a sister but a foundress. This thought brought a great cloud over her soul. Sometimes her courage would fail and she would feel as if she were trapped in a tunnel of fear. In her free moments she would write anxiously to her trusted friend, Bishop O'Connor. On May 12, 1889, Katharine wrote: "All these dismal thoughts of mine could not please our Lord. When I am praying in chapel, I try to overcome my selfishness and self-seeking. I look on my life in the future, and try to be cheerful, since you say it is the will of our Lord." A little farther into the letter, she wrote: "Eternity will be too short for me to regret not doing the will of my Creator and my God."

Bishop O'Connor's answer came quickly on May 16, 1889. He told her that her new religious congregation *was* certainly God's will. The bishop's letter injected new courage and hope into her heart. This was not her work, he reminded Kate, but God's. Everything was in his hands. The young woman was again at peace.

Kate's training continued. She learned hospital tasks and classroom teaching alongside the Sisters of Mercy. Being with children again reminded her of summers at Saint Michel's when she and her two sisters had taught catechism classes.

Bishop O'Connor's health began to fail in the summer of 1889. However, this didn't stop him from planning to go to Pittsburgh in November to officiate at Kate's reception of the religious habit. The visit would work in well since he would be traveling to the bishops' November meeting in Baltimore, Maryland. But in the end, Bishop O'Connor was too ill to make the trip. It was Archbishop Ryan of Philadelphia who presided at the ceremony in which Kate also received her new name—Sister Mary Katharine.

Sister Katharine didn't yet know Archbishop Ryan, but she would soon find in him a real friend. He was to become, like Bishop O'Connor, a spiritual father. The Philadelphia archbishop attended the bishops' meeting in Baltimore a few days after Kate received her religious habit. The event was still fresh in his mind as he spoke to the entire assembly of bishops: "I believe that in the last century we could have done more for Southern Blacks and the Indian tribes.... I believe that...slavery and the unjust treatment of the Indians are the two great blots upon American civilization. So do I fear that in the Church, also, the most reasonable cause for regret in the past century is the fact that more could have been done.... Let us now come in the name of God and resolve to make reparation for these shortcomings of the past."

The archbishop then spoke of the simple but impressive ceremony he had witnessed in Pittsburgh a few days before, when Katharine Drexel "knelt...and offered her great fortune, her life, her love, her hopes, that...all she possesses now or shall possess in the future, may belong to God and to the Native and Black Americans. She hopes that other Christian young women may unite with her and thus begin the great work of reparation, and help to make it perpetual."

The bishops nodded their heads and smiled. They agreed that Sister Katharine was beginning a beautiful work for God.

12

A SHARE IN THE CROSS

A week after Sister Katharine received the habit, wonderful news arrived from her eldest sister. Elizabeth was engaged to Walter George Smith, a Philadelphia lawyer. They were married on January 7, 1890 and left for a long honeymoon in Europe.

Other news was not so positive, however. Bishop O'Connor, as ill as he was, was determined to make a trip to Pittsburgh to visit Sister Katharine. His doctors discouraged it, pointing out that the cold climate was not going to help his fragile condition. On January 9, the holy bishop wrote to Katharine with touching honesty: "I feel crushed and forsaken. Only my faith keeps me going. Pray that its support be not withdrawn from me." The novice would never forget those words. Nor would she forget the lessons she had learned from Bishop O'Connor. Katharine prayed that the Lord would spare his life. She and Mother Sebastian traveled to Saint Augustine, Florida, where Bishop O'Connor was staying. His physicians finally gave him permission to return with the sisters to Pittsburgh's Mercy Hospital. The trip was difficult for the bishop, but the sisters hoped that good hospital care would help him recover. Sister Katharine was given charge of his medicines and trays. The time spent with the saintly bishop was a living lesson on how to grow close to God. Sister Katharine could sense his terrible pain, yet Bishop O'Connor suffered silently. He appreciated all that the sisters were doing for him. Truthfully, though, he realized that he was not getting better, and he wanted to die in his own diocese. For this reason, the bishop made the painful trip back to Omaha.

Sister Katharine received word of Bishop O'Connor's death on May 27, 1890. The novice felt loss and panic. Now who would help her with her new congregation? She remembered how peaceful the bishop had been on his bed of pain. How did *he* go on? And now, how could she go on without his help? At this critical point, when Sister Katharine's courage was beginning to falter, Archbishop Ryan of Philadelphia, took her under his wing. He and Bishop O'Connor had been very close friends. Archbishop Ryan traveled to Omaha, Nebraska, for

Bishop O'Connor's funeral. On the return trip, he stopped in Pittsburgh to see Sister Katharine. He found a frightened novice who, in her own words, "simply could not go ahead and found the new congregation of sisters." The archbishop and Sister Katharine sat in the convent parlor and talked, like father and daughter. At one point, Archbishop Ryan gently asked, "If I share the burden with you, if I help you, can you go on?" Katharine looked up at him through her tears and smiled. Hope seemed to surge through her again. "Yes," she said simply. And Archbishop Ryan became a trusted spiritual father to her from that day on.

It had been decided that after receiving the religious habit, Katharine would make public her plan to begin a new religious congregation. While Sister Katharine continued her training as a novice, young women interested in giving their lives to serve the African and Native Americans approached the Sisters of Mercy. They asked to join Katharine. They became postulants and novices for the new community.

In the midst of all this excitement, news from Sister Katharine's family gave her some cause for worry. Elizabeth, on her honeymoon, had become ill in Florence, Italy.

She had received the Anointing of the Sick. After six weeks of recuperation, the bride was fully recovered. She and her new husband continued their honeymoon trip. Soon after, Sister Katharine received word that Elizabeth was expecting a child. The couple arrived home from their European tour on September 7, 1890. Elizabeth didn't feel well, but she and her husband were very excited about the coming birth of their child. On September 24, she became very ill again. Katharine was called to her side. But by the time she reached Philadelphia, Elizabeth and her child were already dead. Louise and her husband received the sad news while they were on a trip. They immediately headed for home.

Elizabeth, with her child in her arms, was laid in a beautiful casket at Saint Michel's. Sister Katharine knelt close to her sister and gazed at her lovely face. *It seems that you will wake up at any moment*, Katharine thought. She prayed in silence and asked for courage to carry the cross of suffering. And the Lord heard her prayer.

Archbishop Ryan soon helped Sister Katharine choose an appropriate site for her new congregation's motherhouse. The location was about nineteen miles outside of

Philadelphia in an area later to be called Cornwells Heights. Sister Katharine bought sixty acres of land. Early in her novitiate, she had been permitted to go to Philadelphia to make arrangements for her new motherhouse. Her Uncle Anthony and Colonel Morrell advised her about finances and architectural matters. They would oversee the building project.

Sister Katharine completed her novitiate training and was just about to begin her retreat in preparation for her vows when she learned some painful news. There had been a Sioux uprising in the area of Holy Rosary Mission. Sister Katharine prayed for the valiant Father Jutz, S.J., and the Franciscan sisters at the mission. She had financed the building of the mission many years earlier in an effort to help Indian families. Now she begged the Lord that no one would be killed. "Please," Katharine prayed, "let the good Father Jutz and the sisters are doing continue."

Holy Rosary Mission was spared. Sister Katharine credited this to prayer and to the personal intervention of a friend of hers, Chief Red Cloud. Katharine and her two sisters had once met the respected chief on a trip to the reservation. He remembered the three Philadelphia sisters who were so concerned about the welfare of his people. Kate had promised to build a school to educate the Indian children, and she did. Chief Red Cloud had not forgotten this gift. He stood up to the renegade Indians and protected Holy Rosary from their attack.

Sister Katharine pronounced her vows on February 12, 1891. She was now officially Mother Katharine, the superior of a new congregation called the Sisters of the Blessed Sacrament. She left the Mercy novitiate with thirteen young women to begin the next chapter of their religious life. It was the start of a wonderful new adventure for the Lord.

13

GROWING PAINS

Excitement mounted among the young women who had joined Mother Katharine. Even the youngest candidate was enthusiastic about being among the pioneers. *What next?* the sisters wondered. Since their new motherhouse was still in the planning stage, they needed temporary housing. The Drexel summer home, Saint Michel's, was unoccupied. The sisters would move in on July 1, 1891. Mother Katharine and Mother Inez, a Sister of Mercy, went ahead to prepare Saint Michel's. Mother Inez, on loan for a year, would serve as novice director. On July 1, ten novices and three postulants arrived.

The young community quickly caught on to the rhythm of daily convent life. There was time for everything: Mass, prayer, classes on the religious life, chores, recreation and relaxation. Each day seemed so ordinary and calm. Mother Katharine trusted and let God lead the way. "Let us peacefully do at each moment what at that moment ought to be done," she suggested.

Before long, friends of Native and African Americans began calling on Mother Katharine. They were coming to request her sisters' help. The first to arrive was Archbishop Janssens of New Orleans, Louisiana. Others followed. *Soon enough,* Katharine thought happily, *we'll be giving laborers as well as money for God's vineyard.*

More and more young women joined the sisters, fired by their love for Jesus and a desire to serve those in need. Their anticipation grew. "When will we begin our mission? What will our first assignment be, to the Indian territories or the South? And who will get to go?" They were anxious to get started.

The horse-drawn wagon bounced over unpaved roads. Two nuns hung on, their eyes focused on the driver. Sister Mary Evangelista leaned over. "I'd talk more," she confessed, "but every time I try to, I get a mouthful of dust!" Mother Katharine laughed. She knew the feeling. She had been to New Mexico before. She was traveling now

"Welcome, Mother Katharine!"

to the very school she had given the money to build.

The sisters arrived at Saint Catherine's to find that the school had been closed due to lack of teachers. Mother Katharine was exhausted, but tired as she was, she set to work. So many children deserved the education Saint Catherine's could offer. The sisters stayed a week and made lists of everything the school needed. Then they returned to Philadelphia. It was time to have a talk with Archbishop Ryan.

"Saint Catherine's is in need of sisters to teach the Indian children, Your Excellency," Mother Katharine said hopefully.

"It's heartbreaking to see such a beautiful little school empty," Sister Evangelista added sadly.

"Couldn't it be time, Your Excellency, for the Sisters of the Blessed Sacrament to begin working among the Native Americans?" Mother Katharine asked.

The archbishop smiled and nodded. "Yes," he said, "begin with Saint Catherine's."

Mother Katharine returned to the convent and gathered everyone in the dining room. "Sisters, we will be taking over Saint Catherine's School in Santa Fe!" she announced with a smile. The sisters clapped enthusiastically. "How many will go and *who* will it be?" Mother continued. "You'll find out very soon."

In the end, nine sisters were chosen for this first missionary assignment. Sister Mary Evangelista and three others boarded a train on Saint Anthony's feast day, June 13, 1894. As the train chugged out of the station, the four pioneers waved bravely, brushing away their tears. A second group of sisters followed one week later. Soon letters began to arrive at the motherhouse. The trip to Santa Fe had gone smoothly, and the sisters had received an enthusiastic welcome. Mother Katharine kept the whole community involved in the project by reading the letters of the missionaries to them.

During the summer weeks, the nuns at Saint Catherine's readied the school for the September opening. They were anxious to have a large group of students to begin, but only nine had enrolled so far.

In early September, Mother Katherine again made the trip to Santa Fe. She arrived at what she called "starlight." It was 10 P.M. All the sisters were sound asleep. Knocking at the front door didn't help, but the wagon driver knew how to get results. He grabbed the rope of the school's large outdoor bell and began to pull vigorously. Within minutes the sisters, along with most of the population of Santa Fe, were awakened. They knew that Mother Katharine had arrived safely.

Mother Katharine met with Archbishop Chapelle during her brief stay. He assured her that he and his priests would visit the families and encourage student enrollment. Since the school itself was progressing nicely and the sisters were happy, it was time for Mother to return to Philadelphia. In a letter to her Santa Fe sisters written from the train, she said simply: "I loved you before my visit, more since my visit and during it." The young missionaries clung to her words. For them, she was an image of the love of Jesus.

In January 1895, Mother Katharine pronounced her perpetual vows in the presence of Archbishop Ryan. She received a silver ring, a symbol of her lifelong love for Jesus. On the inside of the plain band, her motto was inscribed: "My beloved to me and I to him." This was a day of joy. Mother knelt silently in the chapel. She and Jesus had so much to talk about. She began the conversation by offering her thanks to him.

14

SOUTHERN BEGINNINGS

Mother Katharine, lying in bed, was still awake. Should she also be sending her sisters to the South? If so, where should she begin? She kept hearing the voice of her sister, Louise, raving about the beauty of Virginia's farmlands. Property was available next door to Saint Emma's, the large school Louise had built. What if Katharine could buy that property and build a school for young African American women?

But who will come? she asked herself. Mother Katharine quickly answered her own question: *Young women who sincerely believe in education and are too poor to afford it. My sisters will welcome them warmly.* Smiling at the thought, she finally fell asleep.

Mother Katharine lost no time. She and Mother Mary Mercedes soon boarded a train for Richmond, Virginia. From Richmond, the two rode in a horse-drawn coach to the land that bordered Saint Emma's. They arrived at Mount Pleasant, a mansion that had once been a plantation. Mother looked over the property and realized it was ideal. She climbed a small hill and stood gazing down at the river. "This is where I want the school to be built," she said with determination.

With the local bishop's blessing, Mother Katharine bought the property. Constructing the school would take time. Supplies had to be floated on barges from Ohio to Virginia by way of the James River. But that was all right. Katharine returned to Philadelphia happy. One more important item remained. She needed a name for the school. That was the easy part. It would be called Saint Francis de Sales, in memory of her father.

At last, in the fall of 1899, the school and convent were ready. Mother Katharine and the new superior of Saint Francis, young Mother Mary Mercedes, made the trip to Richmond. Mr. Mosby, their hired farmer and new friend, met them at the train station. He looked worried. "Mother," he said softly, "I have bad news." The two nuns looked at him anxiously. Mother Katharine closed her eyes, expecting the worst. "There's been… a…a…fire," the man stuttered.

"Is everything gone?" Katharine asked.

"No, Mother, but it took nearly half the barn."

"We'll just rebuild then," Katharine sighed in relief. Rumor had it, the farmer explained, that the fire was the work of a few unfriendly neighbors. It would not be the last time the sisters experienced opposition to their work.

Mother Katharine and Mother Mary Mercedes were on hand when the furniture was delivered. The two prepared the inside of the convent. It was soon ready for the nine Sisters of the Blessed Sacrament who arrived on July 24, 1899. What joy! The first Blessed Sacrament convent in the South was ready to begin its missionary labors.

On her next visit to Saint Francis de Sales School, Mother Katharine was asked to make a short trip to Lynchburg, Virginia. She and Mother Mary Mercedes were enjoying the scenery when their train made a quick stop at a small station named Columbia.

"Look," Katharine whispered with excitement. "Isn't that a gold cross in the distance? Do you think it could be a Catholic Church?"

"I don't think so," Mother Mercedes replied.

"But what if it is?" Katharine insisted.

"We should find out." Mother Katharine carefully tucked the image of the shimmering cross in her memory.

The sisters had a student from Columbia. They later asked her if she knew about a Catholic church in her neighborhood.

"Yes," the young woman responded, "but it's not used any more." The sisters wanted to find out why. Two days later, Mother Mary Mercedes and Sister Mary of the Sacred Heart took their student as a guide and boarded the train for Columbia. Upon their arrival, the girl led the nuns through the streets to a small church. Sunlight danced off the golden cross that Katharine had seen from the train. The sisters went inside and found a well kept little church, complete with flowers, fresh altar linens, and enough pews to seat 200 people. They learned that the man behind the mystery was Uncle Zach Kimbro.

Uncle Zach, the only black Catholic in the entire town, took care of the church. The wealthy Wakem family had built it many years before. One of their sons, a Sulpician priest, had celebrated Mass there when he came home on vacation. But most of the family members, including the priest, were now deceased. The one remaining relative didn't live nearby. Uncle Zach had taken it upon himself to care for the church. He had never stopped begging the Lord to send a priest.

The Sisters of the Blessed Sacrament contacted the bishop and asked if they could teach religion classes at the little church on Sundays. They also asked if a priest could come at least once a month to celebrate Mass in "Uncle Zach's" chapel. The bishop said yes to both requests and was very pleased. So was Uncle Zach. He notified the entire town that sisters were coming on Sunday mornings to teach religion. "They'll be here next Sunday!" he repeated with delight. Twenty-five children and seventy-five adults came. When a Josephite Father arrived to celebrate Mass, the little church was full. Uncle Zach's prayer had been answered.

15

To the Navajos

"Where will our next mission be?" the sisters wondered. Mother Katharine's thoughts turned to the Navajo nation in Arizona. She had purchased land there in 1896, and the plot included a natural water spring. The next step had been to find priests who would staff the mission that she would build. Katharine had met the Franciscans of Cincinnati who wanted to bring the Gospel message to the Navajos. At her invitation, three Franciscan pioneers, Fathers Juvenal, Anselm and Brother Placid had arrived in Arizona to stay on October 7, 1898.

The Franciscans began their work by learning the Navajo language. Gradually, they produced a *Manual of Navajo Grammar*, the *Gospels* and other books. The missionaries visited their people no matter how hard the travel by horseback and foot.

Mother Katharine visited the Franciscans in 1900, just two years after they had arrived in Arizona. She admired the good work they were doing and continued to give them financial help. "Our Sisters of the Blessed Sacrament want to minister to the Navajos, too," she explained. "I think it's time to begin building a school and convent." Fortunately, her property with the sparkling oasis, bought years before, would be the perfect spot. This first Catholic school among the Navajos would be called Saint Michael's. The Franciscans helped Mother meet contractors and order supplies. Mother Katharine's Philadelphia architect drew up the plans. October 15, 1902, was the day set for the sisters to move in.

Mother Katharine and Mother Mary Ignatius made another long train trip to Arizona in April, 1902. They arrived at Saint Michael's and stared, speechless. "I expected the buildings to be much farther along," Katharine said with a frown.

"Maybe they had trouble bringing in supplies," Mother Ignatius commented. "We're so far away from everything here."

"Patience," Mother Katharine sighed softly. "We really do need a lot of patience."

That summer, Katharine made another trip to Arizona to check on the progress of the construction. Although it rained hard while she was there, the bubbly spring on the property turned to mud. There was no longer any supply of fresh water. Katharine immediately made arrangements to drill for water. "Please pray," she wrote to the sisters in Philadelphia, "that the men drilling find earthly water so that the Navajos may be led to the *living water* that Jesus gives us."

Katharine finally left for Pennsylvania, promising to return to Arizona in October. Back home at the motherhouse, she received a letter from Father Anselm. "Mother, the Navajos are not too happy about sending their children to school," he wrote. "They're used to educating their children within the family. We have some convincing to do." When he ended the letter by asking her to come to the mission for a meeting, Mother Katharine understood.

"If we don't have Navajo students for Saint Michael's, we can't help these dear people," she explained to the sisters. Mother Katharine and Sister Mary Evangelista again boarded the train for the now familiar trip out west. They were readying themselves for a new experience.

The sisters finally arrived at their destination. An outdoor meeting had been arranged, and the Navajos began to gather. The Native people sat on the ground in a circle. The Franciscans and the two nuns joined them. The Navajos' bright, dark eyes and long straight hair were impressive. *How different we must look to them*, Mother Katharine reflected. She smiled to herself. The Navajo men just needed to be convinced that her sisters wanted the best for their children.

The sun blazed as the meeting began. Father Anselm explained why the sisters were there and what their new school could offer to the Navajo children. The men fired questions like arrows into the afternoon heat. "What will our children learn? How will they be treated? Will they have to live at the school? How long will the school year be?" One by one, the sisters answered as best they could.

After two hours, some eyes still looked puzzled. It occurred to Mother Katharine that with all the discussion, the basic question had not been asked: *Why are you sisters doing this for our children?* She would answer the unasked question. "Why are we sisters doing this?" she spoke up. "Because we love your children, too. We believe that they are precious to God. We want to give them an education so that they can grow up to support themselves and their families. We want them to be happy."

"Will they learn practical trades as well?" a father asked. Mother Katharine nodded her head "yes." As the meeting ended, much of the resistance had melted. Some of the Navajo men agreed that the school was worth a try. December 3 was set for opening day. Through the efforts of the Franciscans and the Sisters of the Blessed Sacrament, forty-seven Navajo children became the first students.

16

A DREAM COME TRUE

The train swayed with a rhythm as it sped toward Chicago. Mother Katharine was on her way out West to visit her sisters in Santa Fe, New Mexico, and Saint Michael's, Arizona. Then she would make the long journey to Rock Castle, Virginia. The year was 1904. Katharine rested her head on the seat and closed her eyes. She seemed to be sleeping, but her mind was hard at work. Her sisters now numbered 104. She smiled and whispered, "Thank you, God." Drawing her rosary from a pocket hidden in the folds of her habit, Katharine fingered the beads as her lips whispered Hail Marys.

Bishop Byrne of Nashville, Tennessee, would meet her at Saint Michael's. He was as anxious as the nuns to see Mother Katharine. The sisters were good tonic for the ailing bishop. They were youthful and generous and in love with Jesus and the Church. These were the teachers he wanted for his *dream* school for African American children in Nashville. Mother Katharine continued her rosary, praying for the zealous bishop. She had already donated money for his school. Of course, now he needed sisters. She didn't want to spread her own sisters too thin. On the other hand, she didn't want to miss opportunities to bring God's love to those still waiting. Her petitions were sent heavenward along with the Hail Marys.

The bishop's meeting with Mother Katharine was a success. His poor health, which had driven him to seek the dry climate of Arizona, was amazingly improved. "I have my heart set on your sisters to staff my school," Bishop Byrne said kindly. Katharine mentally scanned her community—all 104 members including herself—and tried to consider the possibilities. "Of course, it will be tight, Your Excellency. We're still small, but we will come and trust that God will help us continue to grow."

The bishop beamed. "There's an ideal property just a few blocks from a large African American community downtown, Mother. Would you come and look at it?"

"Of course," Katharine responded with a smile.

"But it won't be so simple," Bishop Byrne added quietly. "The building and land are owned by a wealthy man who isn't known for his love for people of color. There is, as you know, some racial prejudice in Nashville."

"You mean we will have to work through a third party to arrange the purchase?" Katharine asked.

"I'm afraid so," replied the bishop, "but I want you to have a look at the building and the property first."

"Just let me know when to come, Your Excellency."

After Bishop Byrne's departure, Mother Katharine continued her visit to the convents. In January 1905, she and Mother Mary Mercedes boarded a train for Nashville. They had been notified that the property they wanted to buy was finally up for sale.

The two nuns rode in a closed carriage with the bishop. The driver slowed as the carriage passed in front of the estate. Mother craned her neck to see what she could while the bishop apologized for the secretive ways. It was necessary, he told them, so that the neighbors would not be angry.

Mother Katharine's newest land purchase was soon final. Papers were signed. The total payment was made through a Nashville lawyer. Everything had been perfectly legal and swift.

No one ever admitted how the information had been leaked to the local newspaper, but it was. The article about the sisters' purchase of the property and their plan to open a school for African American girls, though plain enough, was noticed and caused a storm of protest. Mother Katharine was kind but firm. She would go ahead with her school despite the protests.

On May 29, Mother and Sister M. Juliana traveled to Nashville. The sisters moved from room to room through the large house. They made lists of the furniture and supplies they would need for the school and convent. On that occasion, Mother Katharine named the new school. It would be called Immaculate Mother Academy and Industrial School. The opening date was set for September 5, 1905.

The school came to life with Bishop Byrne's celebration of a Mass of the Holy Spirit. Twenty-eight students attended. They were bright and eager. Classes began even though influential people voiced their criticism. Mother Katharine trusted that the Lord would overcome all the obstacles. And he did.

The first school year passed by. Attendance had grown steadily to over 100 students and the building was now too small. Mother Katharine smiled. It was time to contact her Philadelphia architect. He drew up plans, and by the spring of 1907 the new Immaculate Mother Academy and Industrial School was ready.

LOUISIANA ADVENTURES

Three Protestant colleges for African American students already existed in Louisiana alone. But at that time, when racial segregation was still being practiced, Catholic families of color still waited, hoping that a Catholic college would open for their children. Southern University of New Orleans had grown, and neighbors asked Louisiana lawmakers to move the university to the city outskirts. Despite student disappointment, the school was relocated near Baton Rouge. The move left the former campus buildings vacant. A dedicated Josephite priest contacted Archbishop Blenk. "Now is the time for the Church to buy the university property," he explained. "It will soon be auctioned." Mother Katharine received a hasty letter. "Will you come and look at the property? Will you consider starting a university for African American students?"

"Of course," Mother Katharine answered. She and Mother Mary Mercedes left for New Orleans on April 5, 1915. They met with the archbishop and several business-men. One of them, a Mr. McInerney, was willing to buy the property on behalf of the sisters. Mother Katharine smiled. Experi-ence told her that this would certainly be necessary. If neighbors found out that the sisters were planning to open a school for African American students, there would be protests. Katharine and Mother Mercedes had a few hours free one afternoon and went to visit the site. The sisters stepped cautiously inside the main door, stopping at an employees' desk.

"May we look around?" Mother Katharine asked simply.

"Why not?" the man said kindly. "Go ahead."

A couple of northern tourists, he must have thought. He went back to his work without another glance. Meanwhile, Mother Kath-arine and Mother Mary Mercedes threaded their way through every room of the large building. The two nuns were pleased with what they saw. The auction was to be the next day. Mr. McInerney went ahead and bought the entire property for $18,000. Soon the large sign out front would be changed from Southern University to Xavier (pronounced: Zay-vuer) University. The school would be named after the great Jesuit missionary, Saint Francis Xavier.

Repairmen started their work immediately. Mother Katharine announced that classes would begin that fall. As she had walked through the empty rooms, she had found a recent Southern University catalogue left behind in the moving. The sisters studied it and made up their minds to continue many of the valuable courses. This would help students who had not been able to follow the former school to its new location. Then, of course, they would add Catholic courses.

While the white neighbors voiced their complaints about the buyers of the property, school repairs continued. Xavier University opened its doors to eager African American students and the school continued to grow.

Sisters of the Blessed Sacrament began teaching in several parochial grade schools throughout Louisiana, too. They became aware of the destitute situation of many African Americans in parts of rural southern Louisiana. Father Jean Marie Girault, a missionary from France, was their dedicated pastor. He lived among the poor trappers and hunters who labored on the banks of the Mississippi River.

"They say he comes from a noble French family," one of the sisters remarked.

"He's totally committed to his people," another added. "He's a priest, a doctor, a lawyer, a druggist. And more." Enthusiastic voices chimed their litany of praise as Mother Katharine listened intently. Father Girault's church was called Saint Thomas. He traveled to his parishioners up and down the Mississippi River on his boat, which was also called *Saint Thomas*. Mother Katharine was eager to bring Catholic education to Father Girault's territory. He wrote her asking for money to build a church and school for African American Catholics in City Price. She wrote back that she would like to come and visit.

"Mother Mary Francis," Katharine said with a smile, "how would you like to go on a little adventure?"

"Adventure?" the nun asked with a questioning look. "Where?"

"To Father Girault's parish," she replied. "*And* let's insist on a ride down the Mississippi on the *Saint Thomas*!"

❖ ❖ ❖

Mother Katharine and Mother Mary Francis watched eagerly as Father Girault pulled the *Saint Thomas* ashore. Father fired his gun in the air and people began appearing from every direction to welcome their visitors. Their warmth could not dull the pain that stabbed at the sisters' hearts. The schools they saw were shabby dirt floor huts. This was an urgent project. The white people were very poor; the people of color, destitute.

"There is only one way for these dear people to overcome their poverty—education," Mother explained to her sisters back in Philadelphia. She sent a check for Father Girault's church-school, which he would call Saint Paulinus. This was the first of twenty-four schools, many serving as churches, too, built throughout Louisiana by Katharine. She placed two Xavier graduates as teachers in many of the schools and paid their monthly salaries. The people were grateful. *The most important thing,* Mother Katharine thought, *is that their burdens be lifted and their faith grow.*

18

When Saints Meet

Hurrying to answer the motherhouse door, a sister came face to face with a small nun with piercing blue eyes.

"Good day, Sister. Won't you please come in?"

"Thank you," the visitor simply replied as she was led into the parlor.

"Please, sit down."

"I know I'm not expected," the visiting nun explained, "but I would like to ask a special favor."

"Of course, Sister."

"Would it be possible for me to speak with Mother Katharine?"

"I'm sure she'll see you, Sister. May I give her your name?"

"Yes. My name is Mother Cabrini," the little nun responded.

The younger sister rushed off to Mother Katharine's office. "Mother, you'll *never* believe who's here to see you!" she panted.

Katharine smiled. "By the look on your face, I can see it's someone very special!"

"It's Mother Cabrini," the nun excitedly explained, "Mother Frances Xavier Cabrini!"

Katharine's eyes widened. She rose, abandoned her deskwork, and walked crisply toward the parlor. The two women greeted each other. They had never met, but each was well aware of the good work of the other. Each had started a congregation of sisters. Mother Cabrini's sisters were called the Missionary Sisters of the Sacred Heart of Jesus.

"I came to thank you personally, Mother Katharine," Mother Cabrini began, "for taking such good care of the two sisters I sent to Philadelphia. They didn't know anyone here, and you made your home their own. Thank you so much."

"We were only too happy to help," Mother Katharine answered.

The subject uppermost on Mother Katharine's mind at the time was the rule by which her sisters would live. Perhaps Mother Cabrini could offer her some good advice, since the Church had already approved the rule of the Missionary Sisters of the Sacred Heart. "Mother," Katharine asked her guest, "what can I do to hurry the approval of our rule by the authorities in Rome?"

"Why not bring the rule to Rome yourself?"

"I suggest that you *yourself* take the rule to Rome," Mother Cabrini responded.

This unexpected answer surprised Mother Katharine. "Oh...I don't know," she stammered. "I'm the novice director, too. I would be away so long.... I doubt if Archbishop Ryan would ever agree to that."

"Why not ask him?" Mother Cabrini suggested. "You'll never know until you ask."

Katharine followed her guest's advice and asked Archbishop Ryan for his permission to take her rule to Rome for approval. "A splendid idea!" the archbishop enthusiastically answered.

And so Mother Katharine and Mother Mary James set sail for Rome on May 11, 1907. During their stay, the two nuns had a private audience with Pope Pius X. Mother Katharine felt a deep sense of confidence in him. It was as if she had always known him. The sisters left the audience room with the Pope's face etched in their memory. Pope Pius X was proclaimed a saint in 1954, a year before Katharine's own life on this earth would come to an end.

The rest of the sisters' Roman visit went smoothly enough. On July 5, 1907, the Pope granted an initial approval of the rule of the Sisters of the Blessed Sacrament for five years. Mother Katharine and Mother Mary James were thrilled. They sailed back home, arriving in New York Harbor on August 3. Stepping off the gangplank, Katharine whispered a fervent prayer of thanks.

Mother Katharine's great heart held many treasures, one of which was her gratitude to Archbishop Ryan. During many years of her life he had remained a spiritual guide and father. In January, 1911, Katharine received word that the archbishop was not expected to live much longer. She interrupted her travels to her sisters and returned to Philadelphia, where she was permitted to see the ailing archbishop for a short time every day. "You are the foundress and I am the founder with you," the dying man whispered to Katharine, as she held his hand. "I always look on the Blessed Sacrament Sisters as my congregation," he added. Mother Katharine sighed and smiled. "Thank God," she softly replied.

Archbishop Ryan died on February 11, 1911. His funeral was held at Our Lady of the Blessed Sacrament Convent in North Philadelphia, opened by Mother Katharine in 1909. After the funeral, Mother Katharine finally wept. There would be new archbishops of Philadelphia, but there would be only one Archbishop Ryan.

19

SO MUCH TO DO

The year 1912 was a busy one for Katharine and her sisters. Besides the trip to Rome to seek final approval for her rule, there were invitations from bishops to open missions in Columbus, New York, and Chicago. Mother Katharine began with Columbus, Ohio. The opening of a school for African American children there was planned for the fall. Then it was on to New York's Harlem. The July heat was oppressive as Mother Katharine and Mother Ignatius wandered through the tangle of the city's tenement buildings searching for a location for a school and convent.

"I hope we'll be able to lease two buildings so that we can begin our work here soon," Katharine confided as they walked. "Later on we can look for property to build a school and convent."

"The temporary buildings will probably require quite a bit of work," Mother Ignatius remarked with a smile. She was thinking about who would do most of it and could just picture Mother Katharine rolling up her sleeves. The sisters finally settled on two buildings on 134th Street. Katharine leased them and lost no time hiring workers to clean and renovate the houses. She called for a handful of sisters from Philadelphia to handle many of the details that would speed up the project. Mother Katharine worked alongside her sisters and supervised the construction men as well. She labored from morning to night in the grueling heat. The Harlem project was proceeding well when Mother finally gave in to the sisters' suggestions. She would go to their Philadelphia motherhouse for a brief rest.

And brief it was. Soon she was off to Columbus. The new school there was nearly ready for the September opening day. Then it was on to Chicago to begin a convent and school. Complications arose when the building intended for the school was no longer available. Mother Katharine asked the sisters to set up temporary classrooms in their convent, and classes with the 160 children began as scheduled. Next she traveled to Cincinnati, Ohio, where she had received another invitation to found a school for African American children. From Cincinnati Mother Katharine left for the West. It was always a delight to be with her sisters at the Santa Fe mission.

"She's so pale," one nun whispered. "How can she keep up this pace?"

"I just wonder who could talk her into slowing down a bit," said another, shaking her head with concern. "It used to be that she listened to Archbishop Ryan. He was like a father. But now he's gone."

"Basically, Mother just can't say *no* to any bishop who requests our sisters. There's so much good to do. So many needs."

As the sisters continued their conversation, the superior was speaking with Mother Katharine. But this time it had nothing to do with missionary activities. It was about her health.

"Something's wrong," Mother Katharine quietly admitted, as she sat on the edge of her bed. "I feel sick all over."

"Let's get you into bed, Mother," the superior said kindly as she pulled back the covers. The crisp sheets looked so inviting. Mother Katharine slipped in and felt her body relax. *She's really sick,* the other nun thought. *When Mother Katharine goes to bed willingly in the daytime, something is definitely wrong.*

The doctor was called in. He prescribed medications for a cold and minor lung congestion. He also casually suggested that Mother Katharine be moved to the hospital in Albuquerque, New Mexico. Arrangements were immediately made. And Katharine didn't object. At the hospital she was told she had typhoid fever. Mother Katharine looked with pleading eyes at the doctor, hoping, no doubt, that he would tell her he had made a mistake. But it was no mistake. The exhausted woman pulled the sheets up to her chin and closed her eyes. "Well, Lord," she whispered, "it must be your will. I surely didn't ask for this. I feel nothing but peace." Her head fell back on the pillow and she drifted off to sleep. In Philadelphia, the sisters worried, prayed and waited for news.

Eventually, Mother Katharine was able to travel by train back to the motherhouse. Her progress was slow but steady. By the end of the year, she finally felt like her old energetic self. It was a good thing, too. She was just about out of patience. It was time to get back to work. She sent her sisters on new missionary activities and concentrated on the very important matter of preparing her congregation's rule for final approval by the Vatican.

Mother Katharine and Mother Mary Mercedes sailed for Rome again on April 5, 1913. The final approval of their rule was granted on May 15. It was a glorious day for the Sisters of the Blessed Sacrament. The motherhouse buzzed with excitement and joy as the sisters waited for the return of their superiors from Rome. The happy reunion took place on June 29, 1913.

20

A Matter of the Heart

"Our congregation is growing," Mother Katharine announced to the sisters seated in rows before her. Her eyes met theirs. They were so eager, so ready to serve the Lord. And now they were so many.

"In the beginning we were fewer than a dozen. We have been blessed," she continued, "and yet somehow, incredibly, we are never enough."

"I wish we could all be in two or three places at once!" one of the young sisters exclaimed.

"So do I!" the foundress laughed.

Katharine visited each of her convents, schools and missions every year. She traveled by train as near as possible to her destination. When the train went no farther, a horse-drawn wagon bounced her along dusty trails. As the years passed, many of the trails turned into roads, then highways. And eventually, the rough wooden wagons evolved into sturdy little gasoline-run cars and trucks. For Mother Katharine, busy about the Lord's work, the years flew by.

❖ ❖ ❖

It was 1935. Mother Katharine was planning her annual trips to her thirty-four convents. For a moment, she felt weary. But only for a moment. She glanced down at her wrinkled hands. "I think I'm beginning to get old," she chuckled. "I'll be 77 in November. It's hard to believe! But I've still so much to do…."

Evening came. The chapel was empty now. Mother Katharine slipped into her favorite spot behind the altar. She gazed up at the large crucifix she loved. She opened her arms wide until she herself formed a living crucifix. And she prayed. The nun was in deep conversation with her crucified Lord. Sometimes she whispered, at other times she listened to the voice that spoke in her heart. When she left the chapel, Mother Katharine felt peaceful. She had to make a decision about her busy lifestyle. Her health depended on it, the doctors had said. Her heart could no longer take the strain of her rapid pace. Was it time to step aside? Was it time for one of the younger sisters to take her place? Her eyes dimmed with tears. How much she loved this congregation and each sister! She carried them in her mind and heart always. She saw the faces of the children and adults in their missions. How she loved them, too!

This isn't my work, Lord, she silently prayed, *it's yours. It will continue through every one of the sisters who were called by you as I was. Our dear African and Native Americans will be helped long after I am gone.* The pressures seemed to be lifted from her. It was a good feeling. Mother Katharine gathered the sisters and told them simply that she would be retiring to a life of prayer and closer union with Jesus. Another sister would take over the leadership of the congregation. Katharine would spend this new phase of her journey alongside the sisters at the motherhouse. She would easily be found in the small chapel next to her bedroom.

From then on, Mother Katharine's daily lifestyle became totally different. There were no more phones ringing, no urgent letters to answer, no demands for sisters, for new convents, for payment of work done. How did she react to her new circumstances? With much peace and joy. Katharine was very busy in chapel speaking with her Lord. She had done his work willingly all those many years. Now she could enjoy every minute of her time with the most important One in her life.

The sisters elected Mother Mary Mercedes the second superior general of the congregation. Mother Katharine was pleased. She kept informed about the congregation's growth. She was and remained the *first* among them. Who would have imagined that she was to outlive both the second and third superiors general? Mother Katharine would die during the fourth superior general's term of service.

The year 1941 was painful in world history. The Second World War raged in Europe, and the United States would soon enter it with the bombing of Pearl Harbor. But goodness has its own quiet way of soothing and healing suffering and despair. And Mother Katharine radiated goodness. In spite of all the world's troubles, she deserved to be recognized and celebrated. February 12, 1941, marked fifty years since she had vowed her life to Jesus and founded the Sisters of the Blessed Sacrament. The sisters held a private celebration. On that day Mother Katharine told them: "I just want to say a word to you, Sisters. I thank God that I am a child of the Church. I thank God to have met many of the great missionaries of the Church and to have had the prayers of those great missionaries. I thank God he gave me the grace to see their lives. They are a part of the Church of God. I thank God, like the great Saint Teresa of Avila, that I too am a child of the Church."

A three-day public celebration was planned for April 18, 19, and 20.

"Three days?" Mother Katharine asked, wrinkling her forehead. "Isn't that overdoing it a bit?"

The sisters were ready for her objection. "Cardinal Dougherty has approved of everything," they assured her.

"Oh," the elderly nun said softly, "Well, then, go ahead."

April 18 dawned. The cardinal of Philadelphia, as well as bishops and priests from all over the country had arrived. Groups of young people came. They were students of the Blessed Sacrament Sisters. Pueblo and Navajo Indians danced in their native dress. The Xavier University music department performed a scene from the opera *Carmen*. Students from Rock Castle, Virginia, to Chicago, Illinois, to Santa Fe, New Mexico brought their music and enthusiasm to the celebration. It was their way of saying *thank you* to Mother Katharine and her sisters.

21

"DO YOU SEE THE CHILDREN?"

The years had been gentle to Mother Katharine. She had always been easy to approach. The students of the Sisters of the Blessed Sacrament had never been afraid of her, even though they realized that she was very important. As the days of her life passed by, and Katharine outlived many of her generation, she was peaceful in spending her quiet life of prayer with Jesus.

"When I was young," she said one day, "I suspected I might have a religious vocation." She leaned her head back on the pillow and smiled. "I was right, wasn't I?"

"Oh, yes, Mother. You *were* right," a sister said patting her hand.

"You know, I saw myself as a cloistered sister. I wanted that so much. But Bishop O'Connor helped me to realize the needs of our African and Native Americans. He showed me that helping them was God's will for me. I was so afraid, and yet God was there for me. With each fearful step I took, he walked by my side. That was long ago.

And our congregation has grown. So many people have been given the light of the Gospel through our mission. This is all God's work, his plan, his mercy. He's giving me right now what I wanted most: a life of prayer and quiet with him. He is inviting me to prepare myself for heaven." She sighed happily as the nun beside her bed waited. But no more words came. Mother Katharine was asleep.

Louise, Katharine's youngest sister, died suddenly on November 5, 1943. Kate's journey, though, was not yet over. She would remain twelve more years on this earth. During the quiet hours that made up her daily life, she remembered those who asked for prayers. She called on the Lord to help each sister in her work for him. She prayed for peace in the world and justice for all God's people. Her rosaries were clusters of Hail Marys offered for so many needs and intentions. But sometimes, the elderly nun would just lie still, waiting for the night nurse.

"Are the children warm enough?" she would anxiously whisper. "You can take this blanket. It's so warm. Give it to that poor little fellow over there. I don't need a blanket." Mother Katharine's dark eyes would fill with concern.

"Don't worry, Mother," the nurse would kindly answer. "The children are warm and well cared for. In fact, they're all sleeping peacefully."

"Thank God," Katharine would answer with a sigh. "Thank God."

One evening a sister stopped in Mother Katharine's room. The foundress stared without blinking at the corner of the ceiling. She was smiling. Slowly she turned to the silent sister. "Do you see them?" she asked.

"See who, Mother?" the bewildered nun asked.

"The children," Mother Katharine replied.

The next morning Katharine was still excited about what she had seen. Pointing up to the ceiling, she told a visiting sister, "Oh, all the children were there, all going past, so many of them. And the Pope was there too, and so many children." It was as if Mother Katharine could see the good her congregation had done and was doing for the Church.

From out of the past came the sure, clear voice of Bishop O'Connor. She could hear him again speaking to her about the call to religious life. *It's all right, Kate. It's like an in-*

vitation to a wedding; you don't have to take it if you don't want to. But if you do, it may mean that thousands of people will know God who otherwise could never have known him.

"You were right," Mother Katharine whispered softly. "God sent you and Archbishop Ryan. I owe you both so much. I feel I will be seeing you very soon."

With many sisters gathered around her, Mother Katharine Drexel died peacefully at 9:05 on the morning of March 3, 1955. She had made a total gift—of all that she was and all that she had—to God and to the Native Americans and African Americans whom she loved so much. Mother Katharine would have been 97 years old that November.

A long line of people filed slowly past the open coffin in the convent chapel. Visitors continued streaming in throughout the night. Katharine's funeral was held in Philadelphia's Cathedral of Saints Peter and Paul. Children and adults from all over the country came to thank Mother Katharine one last time and to pray for her.

Philadelphia's Archbishop O'Hara came up to the sisters after the funeral. "You see," he said, "even this cathedral is not large enough for her funeral."

Mother Katharine was buried in a crypt at the motherhouse of the Sisters of the Blessed Sacrament. Just forty-five years later, on October 1, 2000, Pope John Paul II proclaimed her a saint. She is the second native-born United States citizen to be canonized. Her feast day is March 3.

Mother Katharine was the last living member of the Drexel family. At her death, the remainder of the family fortune was divided up and given to the charitable organizations that had been specified by Mr. Drexel in his will, which had been drawn up long before Katharine founded the Sisters of the Blessed Sacrament.

PRAYER

Saint Katharine, there's so much I can learn from you. Even though many persons today act as if money is the most important thing in the world, you show me that it isn't. It's people who are more important than anything else. And you teach me how to treat them with care, compassion and love, just as Jesus would.

I want to become as unselfish as you were, Saint Katharine. It's not always easy, so I need your help. Ask Jesus to show me how I can use the gift of my own life to make the world a better place for everyone. Thank you, Saint Katharine. Amen.

GLOSSARY

1. **Congregation (religious)**—a society of priests, brothers or sisters approved by the Church. The members live together in community, make public vows and carry out some form of service for the people of God.

2. **Crypt**—an underground area used as a burial room.

3. **Foundress**—a woman who begins a new religious congregation or order.

4. **Habit**—special clothing worn by members of a religious community.

5. **Mite**—something very small.

6. **Motherhouse**—the main convent of a religious congregation.

7. **Nitroglycerine**—a liquid explosive.

8. **Novice**—someone who is getting ready to make his or her vows in a religious congregation or order. A novice experiences the life of the community and studies its rule.

9. **Novitiate**—a special time of training for those preparing to make vows in a religious community. The actual *building* where this instruction takes place is also called a novitiate.

10. **Pleurisy**—an inflammation of the membrane around the lungs that can cause breathing difficulties, coughing and dangerous fluid buildup in the lung area.

11. **Postulant**—a person taking his or her first steps in religious life.

12. **Racial segregation**—the practice of keeping members of one racial group separate from another. This is done by preventing persons of different races from attending the same schools, using the same public transportation, etc.

13. **Reformation**—a sixteenth-century movement that began as an effort to rid the Catholic Church of serious problems and abuses but ended in the division of Christianity and the beginnings of the Protestant churches.

14. **Skullcap**—a small round cap worn by Catholic abbots, bishops, cardinals and the Pope. The Pope's skullcap is white. Cardinals wear red skullcaps. The bishops wear

purple, and abbots (the name given to superiors of certain monks) wear black ones.

15. **Superior**—the person who governs a religious community of priests, brothers or sisters.

16. **Vow**—an important promise freely made to God. Members of religious communities make the vows of chastity, poverty and obedience.

BOOKS & MEDIA

The Daughters of St. Paul operate book and media centers at the following addresses. Visit, call or write the one nearest you today, or find us on the World Wide Web, www.pauline.org.

CALIFORNIA

3908 Sepulveda Blvd, Culver City, CA 90230	310-397-8676
935 Brewster Ave., Redwood City, CA 94063	650-369-4230
5945 Balboa Avenue, San Diego, CA 92111	858-565-9181

FLORIDA

145 S.W. 107th Avenue, Miami, FL 33174	305-559-6715

HAWAII

1143 Bishop Street, Honolulu, HI 96813	808-521-2731
Neighbor Islands call:	866-521-2731

ILLINOIS

172 North Michigan Avenue, Chicago, IL 60601	312-346-4228

LOUISIANA

4403 Veterans Memorial Blvd, Metairie, LA 70006	504-887-7631

MASSACHUSETTS

885 Providence Hwy, Dedham, MA 02026	781-326-5385

MISSOURI

9804 Watson Road, St. Louis, MO 63126	314-965-3512

NEW YORK

64 West 38th Street, New York, NY 10018	212-754-1110

PENNSYLVANIA

Philadelphia—relocating	215-676-9494

SOUTH CAROLINA

243 King Street, Charleston, SC 29401	843-577-0175

VIRGINIA

1025 King Street, Alexandria, VA 22314	703-549-3806

CANADA

3022 Dufferin Street, Toronto, ON M6B 3T5	416-781-9131